# Wanting Only

Lyn McCredden

# Wanting Only

*Wanting Only*
ISBN 978 1 76041 518 1
Copyright © text Lyn McCredden 2018
Cover image © Joseph Moncada, used with permission of the artist

First published 2018 by
**GINNINDERRA PRESS**
PO Box 3461 Port Adelaide 5015 Australia
www.ginninderrapress.com.au

# Contents

| | |
|---|---|
| Wanting Only | 7 |
| Winter Gifts | 8 |
| Autumn Night, Northcote Hill | 9 |
| Fig Tree | 10 |
| Pool Dreams | 11 |
| Poets up North | 13 |
| In the Sunny Air | 15 |
| As Anticipated | 16 |
| Eye's edge | 17 |
| Imaginary Boys | 18 |
| Resolution, 1969 | 19 |
| Vacation Experience | 20 |
| Misreadings | 21 |
| Activating Bodies | 23 |
| The Plump Woman's Moon Song | 25 |
| Soft and Sweet | 27 |
| Postmodern Views | 30 |
| A Life in Spam | 33 |
| Returned to Sender | 34 |
| For my next poem | 35 |
| In Aleppo Once | 36 |
| Boat People | 37 |
| Iraq on the Network | 38 |
| Fitzroy Villanesque | 40 |
| TV Dinners in Australia | 41 |
| Going to Bhutan | 44 |
| Nimbin '97 | 45 |
| Old Friend | 47 |
| Resurrection | 48 |
| Nick's Poem | 49 |

| | |
|---|---:|
| Indifferent Angels | 50 |
| Dionysis Dies | 51 |
| Facing South | 52 |
| Your face | 54 |
| Unautobiographical | 56 |
| Word-knots | 59 |
| Gelassenheit | 62 |

## Wanting Only

        Finally, never conceding  
myself, there is  
        nothing after all  
of you, my love.  
        No matter. The world –  
pious suicide – devours its own  
        fingers and toes, reaching  
for the cataclysm – this I – crouching here  
screened off, viewing  
        the flickering wars  
intangible texts, wanting only  
        fathers, sons, lovers  
blown apart, blown  
        away, this ecstasy  
I must not weep  
        for so simple an event  
as your retreating form  
        the smell of your foreignness  
still on my finger-tips  
        that frantic ocean  
my heart hurtling  
        explosive at your shore  
– its purity, its utter islandness –  
the torn world dreams  
        of reaching, finally.

# Winter Gifts

Tonight I am lit
by Neruda's blue stars
and admit to being
a voluptuary of night scents,
cool-breathing daphne,
pittosporum, and creamy freesia.
I roll in the soft moon green
of imagined hillsides,
am brushed by flickering wings,
feel in my fingers
the buzz of simmering burrows.
I crouch in the fig tree's arms,
her silver candelabra,
her water-green tips
tenderly igniting for the black sky,
for the seasons turning,
not random or rare,
but familiar as dream.
Arms full-stretched, hands open,
I'm laughing out loud, in a shower
of winged and shimmering gifts.

# Autumn Night, Northcote Hill

The cool air's diffusing summer heat
and a fat gold moon is an acre wide
in the jet sky.
Here on the hill, it is an urban orchard
where the polyglot crops of exiles
bear fruit in tumbling Federation gardens,
for a race of new consumers.
Now, thick old fig trees
weight their silver branches
with oozing fruit;
and pomegranates, olives and cactus,
high rusty pear trees and almonds
creamy white in their rotten pods
cover the hill.
The Greek grape is neat and netted
beside next door's curling,
Anglo-Saxon apricot,
each one the seasoned voice
of far-off places
and past promising harvests.
Now, you can reach up for the fruits,
biting the familiar flesh,
tasting a century of seasons
churning in the sweet, nurtured juice.

# Fig Tree

Your fat green hands clap in the wind,
rasp, clatter, part.
Breathing light across the lawn
you are a bird heaven,
a backyard jam factory
fermenting your juices,
oozing and sweet.
I am the dapple queen beneath.
You make for me, in your spreading arms
a picture, a place, a world.
There are stories you tell,
from a long sunlit memory
of women in wide straw hats,
sipping tea and whispering
secrets in your shade,
of children who peek, laughing Pans
hopping through the branches;
of mothers making endless jam,
sticky to the elbows.
You are memory.
When all knowing disappears,
when fears grip,
you smile the seasons at me,
silver or green.
I circle round you, branching totem,
transformed in your moving light,
enchanted back
into the living stream.

# Pool Dreams

for Northcote pool goers

Love is in the air,
John Paul Young's dissolving sound waves,
bodies melting, rhythmic,
in the warm, sheltered pool.
Eagle-rocking oldies, aerobic against death
bob apologetic in one small corner.
Tiny faces laughing, gulp
bright air and water,
'I can swim, look, I can,'
while wheelchairs move to the edge,
old, awkward limbs spinning
on rubber rings,
'We're learning again.'

Wet, relieved of gravity,
they are released
into this promised weightlessness,
intimate, enfolding.
Throw yourself into its arms,
this place for mothers and their water babies,
water wings, fluoro foam rafts
and green-frog goggles.
'Look, I'm floating.'
Butterfly and shark,
soundless bombs and underwater ballet,
white legs disappearing into the blue,
a constant stirring of the waters.

Go down into the pool
and there you might meet
the old frog-man,
marshy ancestor with stunted arms,
sharp teeth gobbling,
straining the rich slime,
who rises up before you,
dropping scales and gawp,
pushing aside millenniums of air
and weight and grief,
lifting off then,
laughing, wings arched
incredulous, to the light.
'Look, I can, I can.'
Love is in the air,
the beckoning rebirth
we glide towards
in our wettest, purest dreams.

# Poets up North

for Dorothy, Dorothy, Gig and Silvana

You saucy little wenches,
Sydney tarts, all lush and sweet,
eating and driving too fast
with mouths full to popping
you make love at the lights,
red and green,
under the moon, under the sun.

We don't do that here,
not supposed to.
It's wit and a twist of irony
and *quod scripsi scripsi.*
Passion's in the knowing here,
in the cool quip
and composure,
sedate, green and savoury Melbourne.
The avant-garde is guarded here,
mates everywhere
mysterious and precise
as initiates.

It's not that this is believable,
but there is our climate,
and your bright blue bay's
white light, girls in hot cars
driving themselves,
and further north
the devil's in nature,
fruit falling plump
into your gaping mouths.

It's cooler here,
analytic, theorised,
words clipped and vetted,
the life of art arranged
in buttonholes, nosegays,
and crystal bowls.
And you sprawl away up there,
loose words, loose-limbed,
still a bit counter-culture,
blowing up the skirts
of our southern precisions
with a gush of hot air.

# In the Sunny Air

Years from now, still standing in sunny air,
you're holding something precious in your hands.
Leaning, contented, by your side there,
someone's smiling; around you light expands.
The camera's keen now, but unprophetic,
and cannot tell me what it is you hold
so tenderly. It's your fragile secret
furled in the future. But it makes you bold:
blue, bright eyes still look back, direct, assured,
reflecting open skies, a blessedness
you share with all you touch, unconfused
by tawdry prizes, this world's injustice.
The treasure you hold in the sunny air
is beyond time: shimmering, just and fair.

## As Anticipated

Counting days down
        islands in a long green archipelago
coming for you
        sea mists    sand drifts
in the long tunnels of warm air
        the Pacific moon speckled
on inky seas
        dotting every 'i' on this page
with the precision of tears
        the common, exact physiology of grief
from belly    to chest    to mouth's 'O'
        and then the eyes, these soft pearls
in my hands, seeds
        I'll scatter, palms up
                          to the four winds.

# Eye's edge

At the eye's edge
his black form
severe late Rothko
manoeuvring
against the light
manifesting this gait
she has known
this misleading solidity –
palpable shoulders
block of torso
dark obliquity –
monumentalised by her
hot head
shattering mirrors
to get to him
somewhere outside
the superimposing frame
the crooked blinding halo
of her light-tricked eyes

# Imaginary Boys

for Ron, reading David Malouf

Your boys are all delight,
slim-hipped deers or godlings
who slither through your dreams,
separated from your day self, made up
of mist and marsh and ether.

Your words are the fine nets,
light, sticky gossamer
thrown out across the gulf
for their boyish, migrating forms.
The shock, the joy of their capture!

Knowing them for the first time,
you find connections
which are terrible and untrue,
erotic phantasmagoria.

I wish you all the boys –
all the beginnings, the fresh starts –
your dreams can make for you,
your small, strong, writer's hands
cupped, unfurling, thirsty
for the sweet stream Ovid tasted.

May your little band of feral boys
go on dancing at the edge
of water, light and words,
eternally uncatchable.

# Resolution, 1969

As if a breaking heart
                         could clip the moon
and thoughts be anything        but moody
gusts, pitching
                waves hissing on a green ocean
the body's minefield of loss and longing,
its passions – impatient children – rushing
                at the earth's corners,
to take their first steps – innocents – laughing and
untouchable,
the audience watching     in rapture,
walking on the moon     the world agog,
eyes lighted globes             moonstruck
for Peace, picture perfect           as if
that perfect baby could really be delivered gently into your arms
all Child      all beauty and softness there
at your fingertips       and you
the fulcrum of air and fire
       unscathed and burning
               with inconceivable, immaculate resolution.

# Vacation Experience

A sexual tourist
morphing in his bed,
for his eyes and mouth,
he, *en vacance* in a loud shirt,
she, tracing herself, stalking
the outline of a new shape
and the taste of him, salt and storm,
an embracing ocean on the tender
edge of the tongue,
but only for *The Experience*
without bomb blast, world change,
just the tropical paradise
you take on and off
a cheap T-shirt, Che Guevara
smiling up approval from the bathroom floor,
water steaming him back into neutrality,
her deranged limbs no longer needed,
rearranging themselves for home.
But it can't be the same
now you have the memory
or at least the promo
for something bigger than vacation
ravenous, unfulfillable –
her shivering need
shrinking in his eyes,
he, always just a blink away
from reclaiming his proper face.

# Misreadings

I am in the back country, cruising green roads
looped with fruitless vines
withering, old,
the peering eyes of faces
that should be readable.
So I play cartographer, turning flat signs
into true-blue greetings: his cagey smile
transformed into passionate collusion.
Embarrassingly, when you begin mapping,
it's the clichés that get you going:
it's Deliverance Country,
and you're on a quest (oh yes,
there is a narrative!) to eradicate
abject voyeurism.
You are not just a tourist
because you can turn words
into pulsating matter, here in this back-country.
But the trip soon bogs down,
the river's source untraceable in this flood.
Still, you are the map-maker, the trailblazer,
semiotician in a swaggering hat
and unstoppable limousine,
so you drive past derelict road blocks,
insisting that your heart – that incendiary –
knows the way. You will make familiarity
where none exists. You will pivot nonchalant
round the next corner and there it is:
the river's source – fresher, cleaner, baptismal.

Is it utopia beckoning on the horizon,
your montage friend calling
your intimate nickname,
or just your hopeless over-reading?
No matter, it's all done
to the sound of breaking glass
as you miss the bend
and go crashing through the undergrowth again,
bull in a china shop, he said.
But all those eyes, half-bored in the bushes,
look away, blank, refusing your brand
of travelling theory.
You should have stayed home
(no Anna Karenina, not even Emma Bovary),
screwing your ideas and your driving skills
back onto the page, waiting,
flat map abandoned,
pouring over someone else's
violet hour.

# Activating Bodies

for Liz Grosz

Your activated body leaning
home the point,
caresses, firms
the Big Questions,
large-boned hands cupping
a chin atilt in quest mode.

You refuse all middle men –
the bi-s, the reactors,
Darlinghurst queers
from comfy suburban bolt-holes
who, for their stylish otherness,
their short-cut, ear-ringed cool
pay nothing –
and you demand, priestess,
of yourself first,
and of this pliant generation,
a New Body
pressing forward,
a future body, laughing at itself
and pleased to laugh with others
in a labile dance of joy,
partnering itself and any
who touch it, spinning with you
beyond the petrifying now,
perpetually ahead of yourself.

Of course I want this,
to overreach
these sagging conformities –
our old, inherited selves
and sexual habits,
that ageing missionary position –
to partner the world
in a long jouissance,
political and pleasured all at once (!),
cutting edges with abandon,
doing what my body never did,
new and free-form
flying.

But it's no place for the weak,
this volatile postmodern forge
to which you draw us, priestess,
offering new wine

to clenched fists,
seducing, intoxicating
with your cup of potent blessing,
constructing minds and bodies
powerful enough
for resurrection.

# The Plump Woman's Moon Song

My body's moon-fed
dimpled round,
my glowing lunacy
an appetite,
gargantuan, pear-ripe.
I am a harvester!
Oh, the streets I silver over,
the suburbs and straight cities
by their shining bays,
the sailors I would devour!

My knees drop open
in season,
drawn apart by tides,
the sea filling me,
the plankton-woven, the rushing ocean,
the push and weight of all the salt waters
scour me, purging
limbs and the hollows between
of my roundness,
my fantastic body.

And ancient as the moon
and still, the season falls,
its dark threads
glistening, wound round
my hurting shadow,
fingering the last fruit,
hollow and dry,
the perfect red and empty
mouth of pain.

You, moon, pare me down.
You stare at me.
Your gold grin knife-
thin and glass-sharp,
carving me up,
gazing, incanting
your One Woman song:
for the Rubenesque
and the anorexic,
the fecund, the paranoid,
and all women
under your insatiable command.

Remembering my next resurrection
I cradle my pale, warm belly,
womanly, rounding
like the next big moon.

# Soft and Sweet

'One body, manipulable, divine,
Outside my head, voices, none of them mine.' – Anon

Sonia's soft and sweet –
a spongecake –
Pammy's plump and ripe.
Sue is small and suckable,
Jen juicy,
Elle edible,
Dee luscious.
'And Marilyn,' the radio jockey whispers,
'Do you want to know what I really think about Marilyn?
She had a big bum!'
Oh, thank you for that,
thank you for tearing another flap
of cold, dead myth off
and showing us again
the warm and wanting flesh below.
That's Marilyn all right,
immortal, remouldable
plump white thighs.

And here is Sylvia,
sculptor of a thousand bodies –
'flayed, transparent,
invisible, distended',
hair, teeth and hands
of a colossal form
in which she could not hide,
which would not hold her.
The Estate took in hand her nasty bits,
the gross gobbets of gossip,
the sinusitis and menstruation pain,
the blood-filled shoes,
serving up for culture
Sylvia phoenix,
self-transcender.

When mummy feeds her little boys
top full of mummy's love,
she oh so slowly understands
that she's the feeder, and the food.

And heeere's the lovely Deb.
Doesn't she look great?
Give her a hand!
And what've you got for us tonight, Deb,
beside your lovely self?

Hey, Denise, you've got a great future ahead of you!
It's all up front for you now, darling.
No back ache, I hope!

In culture's workshop,
the armoury of front and back,
the body tops and bottoms,
lips and hips and scarlet fingernails
lined up for duty.
They've seen it all,
been it all –
Hollywood starlets and royal wives,
page threes and strippers
and sweet sixteens,
anorexics and rich, large women –
been screwed on, stripped off,
fattened and sweated and starved.

The clientele aren't exclusive.
All come, naked, in need,
with their director, prince,
editor, pimp or parent
whose large, round eye wanders
over racks of flesh and shapes
unsatisfied, voracious,
a girl in someone else's image:
trembling, plump, delicious,
dying for consummation.

# Postmodern Views

The way I view it
self-absorbed, sadly,
the old dream of meaning
turns slowly, waves and disappears
through a closing door –
a film door, a dream door,
the thousand-frame TV door –
while muscle-men bounce it at the entrance,
strobes and private school girls inside,
the long recession a real black
turn-off, outside.

I slouch in the vestibule,
longing for it as it goes.
The bouncers are tight
ham-fisted functionaries,
their academic sureness
and my bleeding heart
partners in a postmod sitcom,
a disco of revolving panels,
being all things, in all positions,
without the missionary zeal.

Wittgenstein, watching from philosophy,
writes a long version
of the script in himself,
from *Tractatus* to *Investigations*;
Eliot reverses the order,
repossessing hope along the way,
while Gertrude and Alice speak
in other tongues, trading on hormones
for their place in the dance,
and White's idiots stand along the walls,
grinning extras in their author's
loud and lordly absence.
Right down the century,
see-sawing, we've prepared,
running at it:
'*fin de siècle*' titillating
like a half-shut door,
transvestites embodying it all,
postmoderns pointing to
the 'thing-that-cannot-be
in-itself'.
And women once again
are 'not fragmented',

not hacked pieces
but 'parodies of fragmentation',
cleverer than their masters
they hope, undressing madly,
madonnas all,
for another go at nudity,
this time with every door open,
all exposed like nothing,
the farewell scene a send-up
of *Gone with the Wind*
by Fast Forward,
shot in dream sequence
for popular consumption,
self-styled oysters
for the multimillion gullets.

Or yet again
a new opening
for the same old muscleman
with a soft heart and watery eyes
looking for gaps in the programme,
another go
at touching up,
tricking out
the fading black and white,
the shapeless fuzzy bit part
exiting through a slot
in the scenery
with bad reviews?

# A Life in Spam

14th QS-Apple Conference, click here,
click here, Spaforlife, Lastminute
deals, Booking.com for Berlin,
Sydney Valletta Firenze Lecce,
Your skin solution for a Younger
Facebook added a photo
Of people I don't want to see,
Extended Deadline CFP
T2 Tea, Info@globe, CSAA-forum
ASAL News, Trybooking Team,
the next need Expedia
about.me, mylocalsalon
Brazillica, Ticketmaster
with no where to go
fr. $62 p/n Melbourne package,
Dine in Style Rushcutter's Bay,
The Age subscription overdue,
CFP This is my City, but
you are elsewhere, turned off
and choked with longing
for RealLife.com

# Returned to Sender

Host unknown,
host not found.
Arrival-Date: Mon,
1 May 2000 20:22:07 +1000 (EST)
Final-Recipient: RFC822;
Action: failed
Status: 5.1.2
Remote-MTA: DNS;
Diagnostic-Code: SMTP; 550
Host unknown
Host not found.
Last-Attempt-Date: Mon,
1 May 2000 20:22:33 +1000 (EST)
Return-Path: mail undeliverable.

# For my next poem

Yesterday I saw you in the mall, a battler,
signing up for *The Britannica*,
'$2,000 for a lifetime of knowledge'
and debt to the book company.
It looked a hopeful acquisition:
you, smiling and blushing,
he, suited, courting to replace
all those scrimping, mothering, bookless years
when every salesman knew more than you,
and your kids grew taller,
correcting and informing petulantly.
And I stood registering
the greed of ignorance,
the empty, hungry, common need
consuming you.
All this I noted semiotically,
well-fed by Marxist theory and postmodernism,
stung by the pleasure of an image
for my next poem.

# In Aleppo Once

No more soft words, no intimate whispering,
only the crack of thrown pearls scattering –
machine-guns blistering the bloodied tribes
of Syria – while we Turks and Venetians,
all voyeurs and connoisseurs, peer untouched,
blank eyes that cannot be subdued by tears,
prone beneath our fake Arabian trees,
quite glutted in our melting moods, pens raised,
consumers ogling unpoetic views,
crouching beasts digesting the nightly news.

# Boat People

June 2002

You can smell the warm continental air
calling them, each one, across ancient seas,
touching one man's cheek, riffling a child's hair,
rocking this ark of aborted histories.

Shadows of the new land flicker, dancing
in tired, fevered eyes, a festival
of riotous freedoms so entrancing
they do not hear the ocean's dying fall.

Such lawless romance must be refused.
Small lives should stay in line, should know their place.
The land of sweeping plains is unconfused,
its hard horizons offering no grace.

# Iraq on the Network

Part of a vast armoury
lumbers to life on the network
from an antique land, and sandstorms
blow up the noses of freedom fighters –
Sgt Hank from Arkansas, and Pete
from Kooeerup, and Tony's Irish boys –
while bits of the map slip off the screen
and Leunig's Mother of all Bombs
rips towards a mother of three
trudging across her horizon
in the arms of Allah,
and the good ol' boys grip the Bible
and John H. War in his simple man's speech
licks the holy fundament of the USA
and everyone's narrative impatience
declares it's time and something
must give to feed the maw
of little men choking on gigantic ideas
and the world's moment
of truth and headlines.
And isn't it exciting
– not since Vietnam – but this time
we'll get it right and the approval rating
is going up, because something's happening
and that's more dazzling than nothing,
and the Clifton Hill train station graffiti reckons
women should be in charge 'cos
they could stop the war and breastfeed
at the same time. Imagination stumbles.

The story collides with children
and mothers and toughened young men,
and water storage facilities and schools and electricity plants,
old roads threading through ancient Baghdad
and manly laughter and dancing
with brown-eyed, black-haired children agog
with sleepiness and tired play, and sweet fruit
scrunched in their hands without fear
because the summer is coming
and the air is warm and humming
with promise.

# Fitzroy Villanesque

Since ecstasy is no one's given right,
mooching and drifting, waiting for the call,
you haunt this shabby suburb late at night.

Each small exuberance has taken flight,
night rolling in, a shrug, a dying fall,
and ecstasy is no one's given right.

Lean forms slither, black and blue through light,
leave no redeeming palimpsest, no scrawl,
haunting this shabby suburb late at night.

Your muffled cries, your shuffling feet, ignite
only small flames, memories half-recalled,
since ecstasy is no one's given right.

Waiting for that beloved shape, that light
which can draw you, spectre, past these black walls,
you haunt this shabby suburb late at night.

You hear again – fingers trembling – how bright,
how warm that welcome voice, and its withdrawal.
Since ecstasy is no one's given right,
you haunt this shabby suburb late at night.

# TV Dinners in Australia

In memory of those who died in the Hillsborough soccer stadium crush, 1989

'It will never happen here,' experts say. 'There aren't enough people, and everyone's got a seat.' – ABC News

That grief there,
flat and framed,
looks back at you: the game,
the howls and snorts
of football fans
jammed into tight
small grey square
asphalt airless
visual consumption.

It's like those old telephone-box crowdings,
mini- and volksy-fillings
screaming at the top of your lungs
young, with big bodies
demanding air, legs plump
up and out the window.

Here, you peruse the crying heads,
the metaphors of horror
rising up, and you say,
'The English love a good old bout
of ritual grief, don't they?
Like barracking when you know you've had it.
"You Never Walk Alones"
un-bloody-deniable in that crowd.'
And you say,
'It's women who always cry.
Look, here she goes again, son,
bawling at the telly.'
And the viewer says,
'Unnecessary really, all those close-ups.
Do eat up, before it goes cold.'

What could it ever mean,
all those earthbound boys,
the dreary contortions of dead enthusiasts?
Better imbibe just enough,
see, but not believe.
You'd better chew and digest discreetly,
or you'll choke on it:
Biafra, Beirut,
Bopal, Bradford,
Baghdad,
and a small suburb in Liverpool.
No ripping flesh with overt hunger,
streams of red juice running
down your chin.

'Eat up now or the Chinese'll starve
and I'll turn that box off!'

Better, really, to switch off quickly,
turn off before it gets tasteless,
untelevisual,
rows of blue shrunken faces
gawking at you
through metal grids
a million miles away.

# Going to Bhutan

The radio says
it's poverty-raddled, the Junta
hate the Hindus, and the Buddhists
are non-citizens, gagged
and barred from their temple.
Over there, a river of refugees
pours out across the desperate world,
as far as Australia.

But they do have
Gross National Happiness
indexed against advertising,
wrestling channels, plastic bags
and traffic lights. Ah, bliss!

While here, misnamed Economy
puts on his fat, leery smile,
pockets crammed with fools' gold,
not happy yet but barging
big-shouldered into a future
undreamed of, where we'll soon know
what we've always wanted,
and grasp it for the first time,
again and again.

So, I am going
to Bhutan, to feel the need.
I want to worship at those shores
of immeasurable, inconsolable grief,
a sympathetic tourist of orphaned,
antique kingdoms, waving
my wad of unhappy dollars.

# Nimbin '97

The myth of you has grown –
fed by your strange crops,
watched over
by those daunting rock sentinels –
beyond your value.
Footfalls echo in your valley.
Orange Kombis still nose towards you
along the Lismore road,
or down the northern river passes,
earnest trippers still 19,
wanting to touch your story,
to catch at the original ecstasy
glimpsed in their parents' eyes
after too much scotch or chardonnay.
It's still there in your perfect green,
your barefoot insistence on One Nature,
benign and succouring.
But like a faded den
deserted by the furies,
the Main Street Museum's psychedelia
promises nothing,
its calculated combo of Joni and Bob
a sing-along prompt for tourists
trailing bored kids already retro,
who can't believe
this dusty propaganda, its priceless slogans:
'Make love…' Yeh, yeh.
'The nuclear family kills.' Is that us, Mum?
'Solidarity with Mabo' another tribal merger.
Nimbin, you're not a place to grow old in.

Undercover idealists feel it most,
embarrassed by their incongruent pasts
balanced precariously
in the well-heeled now.
Or maybe it's your locals,
leather-skinned, wild eyes
expecting nothing. They live on
the scraps we proffer,
surreptitiously, feral dogs
under our groaning tables.

# Old Friend

I choose to live in a mongrel suburb,
my scruffy street a united nations.
You live on the leafy side, unperturbed
by sameness, your own face, your relations.
You tell me, over coffee and éclair,
that on a rare train trip last week you'd seen
'a boy from Footscray, or somewhere out there,
you know, tats, moccasins and stove pipe jeans.
He vomited in the carriage, right there
in front of everyone. Didn't clean up,
just stared round with a stupid grin. "Who cares?"'
The look on your face was not quite disgust,
telling your little western suburb story,
but unamused, self-congratulatory.

# Resurrection

i.m. Seamus Heaney, 30 August 2013

Tonight the news is full of coming wars –
four hundred children lie in tattered shrouds;
these things we know are true from shore to shore.

So, in quiet Damascus, through open doors
the nation's father sends his poisoned kiss,
tonight, when news is full of coming wars.

So, far away, in Ireland's song-swept fields
the poet of loss and joy, the shepherd
of things we know are true, must finally yield.

On the wind from ancient desert moors,
to green valleys where peace, surely, persists,
tonight the news of endless coming wars

will not be heard by one whose songs of peace
lie with him – seeds of resurrection,
of things we know are true, and of release.

Sleep well, at line's end, great Irish singer.
Your odes – of beauty, terror, and the earth –
teach us to sing against the coming wars,
of things we know are true, from shore to shore.

# Nick's Poem

Do you get to choose
where you die? he asks,
the Melbourne General slipping past
as we drive for the suburbs and sleep.
You mean 'buried', don't you?
(always safe in words).
Yes, 'buried'. Can you choose?
I want to be buried next to you.
You'll go first, and then
I'll know where to come.
As if he would always be
five years old,
sleep-sweet in the morning
slipping beneath the covers,
warm between parents
who'll go first,
ready for another endless day.

# Indifferent Angels

You see them again,
in dreams or poems,
or in others' faces –
the dead father,
the lost child,
the unloving lover –
and you wonder
if it's for reassurance
or revenge they're sent.
The years stretch out
and you walk through them,
brushing shoulders with these ghosts
who care enough to visit.
Or do they – indifferent angels –
taunt and disperse,
tiny feathered shadows on air,
re-sent through virtual spaces,
simulacra moving you
regardless,
with their blank stare,
their hollow promise.

# Dionysus Dies

for M.H.

Caught in the glittering
                         wide-eyed harbour stare
at your toes and finger tips
                         another gorgeous pill-spray
not even your pale gaunt lady
                         or her pretty, pretty brood
can touch you, lovely
                         deep growling boy face
full-mouthed
                         sweet-hipped
mad limbs spinning
                         tangling in the twist
the rush
                         you have tongued and sung
a rude child leaving
                         as innocent as love
on a whim, on a song
                         raging pleasure
tearing yourself
                         apart.

# Facing South

Up in the Arts tower,
below the south lawn's
smooth hill
and its subterranean carpark,
the class is facing further south
into winter light.
They are doing Donne on death –
*Per fretum feberis* –
digging, desultory, for resonance
half-remembered, or learned
rote in Lit One.
Before the poet's obsessions
their winter faces falter
but are too alive to feel the grip
of hard earth,
the gnarl and drag
of unimaginable history.
Their fresh faces, tricked
pale in the cold light,
already scan for the hour's end,
the next allotment
of learning before lunch.
And who is she
tutoring in ignorance,
to reignite
old Renaissance whisperings?
What can the young do
against such wizened knowledge?

> 'They thought like that, then,
> there was more dying,
> you know, when they were still young.
> The plague, wars, bad sanitation.'

The hour dwindles, uncaring, to its close.
Outside, light shifts
in soft waves, moves
over the emptying room,
not expecting, as it goes,
sympathy or even acknowledgement.
Vacancy braces itself.
10.15 to 11.45,
next class, same topic,
same burrowing blind life
storing up its grains of culture
harvested against stupidity
and the long winter nights.

# Your face

for Robin Grove

I see your face across busy rooms,
or in a street of strangers,
familiar and wry
eyebrows leaping
with the furious farce of it all,
your wet-eyed, wicked enjoyment.

Sometimes I hear your laugh,
generous and knowing,
your confusing irreverence
and awe in quick-step alternation;
your lightning transformations
of joy, from resignation.
You've been gone a year now.
The world is dull and unilluminated.

You moved lightly with your dancer's step
your gracious hands
that knew Mozart and Bach,
soil under your nails,
old-fashioned hymns,
and a child's rounded head.
Your heart was woven with words
– Shakespeare and Donne and Eliot –
words you gave away
to so many
hungry to hear,
words freighted
with humble gratitude,
with rapier élan,
precise and measured pause,
your quicksilver, dancing self.

# Unautobiographical

*Und hast die Welt gemacht. Und sie ist groB*
*und wie ein Wort, das noch im Schweigen reift.*
*Und wie dein Wille ihren Sinn gegreift,*
*lassen sie deine Augen zartlich los…*
– Rilke, *Eingang*

To be the reader/writer proper
of *The Life* – your own –
demands nunnish renunciation,
or severe old age –
dissolving, letting go.
Otherwise, mouthing off too soon,
it will not be what you meant
at all.

Wait, until age relinquishes
flesh melting into itself,
the days rolling towards night
in catnap, dream, or sigh.
Then, writing, surely,
will not be
for status, shield, or show –
unless, still raging for more,
the decrepit ego
scrabbles for immortality.

But now, in the middle,
here on this ridge between
the heat of summer at your back,
commitments shouldered,
and the trek downwards just begun,
there is neither celebration,
nor time for bowing the head.
To complete *The Life*,
delivering it for all it's worth,
would be to glimpse, unmoved,
those others –
shadow-selves, not-you –
disappearing ahead on the lonely path.

Yet already you realise
no body here on the sheer descent
can ever know, ah,
the dreams a child once juggled
in the sunny air;
no one can feel with precision
the lift and stride
your limbs must struggle for,
bone on bone,
before they fall.

But still, the last word
which comprehends us all,
which dreams you,
must now, mid-world,
be unwritable.
The sun warms your retreating form,
shadows blackening along the path –
look, how tall you've grown! –
down to where mere writing
could never be
*The Life.*

# Word-knots

for Scott

Already late autumn
but still warm,
we sat outside
under those perfect trees,
our wine pale gold.
Friends' knowing laughter,
fretting casually about mothers
and work, what could be done,
the bizarre violence of bureaucracies.

Your face was golden brown,
summer's mirror,
round as a nut,
your sleeveless top – a trademark –
your close-cropped hair
not quite proper
in this establishment of Higher Learning
you loved and derided.

I grizzled about the stresses,
the usual tired grumblings –
I wasn't loved enough,
my students seemed unmoved,
I could do better if they cared.
You listened, playing camp mother
to perfection,
hazel eyes intent,
offering the hard word-knots
with which you honoured me,
commanding your stuttering share
of the time.

I still miss your open face,
your comings and goings
at my office door,
that air of long summers
sweeping in with you,
an ageless Puck,
carefully irreverent,
promising to come again.

I won't forget
you once invited me –
it was inconvenient, I was busy –
to visit your new place,
your own fresh, light, breezy rooms.
You had painted them
bright, dazzling, sail-ship white.

It was a celebration.
You served bowls of lollies –
snakes, sherbets and smarties.
There was laughter, and love
and cool kids posturing
that broody summer's night.
You welcomed me
as if I belonged.
I couldn't stay long,
work to do.
You were ravishing among your friends,
a colossal-hearted boy
preparing to fly away.

# Gelassenheit

Waiting, something opens
without our willing it,
without force.
Calm, in half-light, the horizon
crosses our sight,
the opening
of a dawn, a memory,
half-hoped-for
your metaphors coming home
familiar ghosts, dreamed of
as they cross through the loved fields
and dry gullies,
bringing with them unspoken conversation,
new thought suspended
without knowing,
awaited, but unattended.
A vastness of silent notes
accompanies us, a symphony
we have longed to hear
of belief far beyond
our interpretations, open
to the swinging movement, and the resting,
this letting go
between here and any horizon
you have ever dreamed, seeing
the other side
of this surrounding openness
coming to meet us,
this spaciousness which is halted and held,
where everything merges
immeasurable in its own resting.

www.ingramcontent.com/pod-product-compliance
Lightning Source LLC
Chambersburg PA
CBHW062201100526
44589CB00014B/1902